Try *

29  Brownies           100 ml margarine, 2...
30+ Brownies           125   "
30?  Choc Chip Cookies  250ml marg  550ml "      "
*34  Choc Chip Meringe Cookies  1pkg Choc Chip (170gm) 4 egg whites
*36  Date Bars          175ml marg. 375 flour 250 Oatmeal
*38  Date Nut Meringes  4 egg whites
40   Ginger Cookies    200 marg  625 ml flour
41   Peanut Butter Cookies  125ml marg 1egg 250 peanut butter
42   Refrigerator Date Pinwheels 250 marg  375 ml flour
46   Refrigerator Oatmeal Cookies 125 marg, 1egg 1000ml flour
48   Rolled Sugar Cookies 250 mg  2 egg 875 ml flour  200 flour 150 oatmeal
50   Sesame Cookies    200 marg       1 egg  500 ml flour
50   Soft Sugar Cookies 200 marg  2 egg 675 ml flour
Fat 55  Banana Bread    250 marg  4 eggs  1000 ml flour
57   Biscuits           75 mg fat  500 ml flour
*59  Buttermilk Pancakes 300 ml flour  30 ml oil 1 egg
*61  Coffee cake        75 marg  1egg  375 flour
*62  Grapenut bread    250 buttermilk, egg  500 ml flour
*64  Muffins            60 oil  1 egg  500 ml flour
*66  Blueberry Muffins  60 oil  1 egg  500 ml flour
*68  Cranberry          60 oil  1 egg  500 ml flour
70   Popovers                   2 egg  120 ml flour
*71  WW Apricot Bread  60ml oil  1 egg  250 ml flour
*74  Apple Crisp        75 marg  120 ml eval milk  75ml flour
75   Granola Type Cereal  180ml oil
77   Uncooked Raspberry Spread
*79  Fudge              125ml marg, 180 ml evap milk
83   Meat Loaf

# Metric Cooking
# for Beginners

# METRIC COOKING
## for Beginners

by Ginevera Barta

*illustrations by* COLETTE PETERS

ENSLOW PUBLISHERS
60 Crescent Place, Box 301
Short Hills, New Jersey 07078

Copyright © 1978 by Ginevera Barta

All rights reserved.

No part of this book may be reproduced by any means without the written permission of the publisher.

**Library of Congress Cataloging in Publication Data**
Barta, Ginevera.
  Metric cooking for beginners.

  Includes index.
  SUMMARY: Explains how to use metric measurement methods in the kitchen and includes recipes to demonstrate these techniques.
   1. Cookery—Juvenile literature. 2. Metric system—Juvenile literature. [1. Cookery. 2. Metric system] I. Peters, Colette. II. Title.

TX652.5.B264    641.5    78-6737
ISBN 0-89490-009-9

Printed in the United States of America

10 9 8 7 6 5 4 3 2 1

Through the years I have enjoyed teaching beginning cooks of all ages, including Girl Scouts, junior and senior high school students, college students, and adults through the New York State Extension Service. With maternal love and prejudice I dedicate this book to my favorite beginners:

*Ann, Nancy, and Bruce*

# Contents

Introduction to Measurements for Beginners    9
Metric Measurement by Volume    11
    *Equipment you will need*    11
    *How to use metric dry-measure containers*    12
    *How to measure dry ingredients by volume*    13
    *How to measure liquids*    14
Metric Measurement by Mass (Weight)    16
    *Equipment you will need*    16
    *Get acquainted with your scale*    17
    *How to use the scale*    18
Metric Measurement of Pan Sizes    19
Metric Measurement of Baking Temperature    20
Non-Metric Terms    20
Let's Develop Good Work Habits    20
How to Tell When Baking Is Done    21
Recipes Let You Choose Your Method of Measuring    24
Recipes    27
    *Brownies and Cookies*    28-53
    *Quick Breads*    54-72
    *Other Recipes*    73-82
Dinner Menus and Recipes for Beginners    83-86
Kitchen Experiments    87

Afterword for Adults    89
    *About the Recipes*    89
    *Measurement by Volume vs Mass (Weight)*    89
    *Terminology*    91
    *How to Change Conventional Measures*
        *to Metric Units*    91-92
    *Manufacturers of Metric Measuring*
        *Utensils and Scales*    93
    *Addresses for Manufacturers and Distributors*    94

Recipe Index    95

# Introduction to Measurements for Beginners

## Early Cooking Measurement

I have a recipe written by my grandmother (probably during the late 1800's) which calls for "butter, the size of an egg" and "a handful of sugar." You can find old recipe books that call for all sorts of odd measurements such as butter, the size of a filbert, hazelnut, butternut, walnut, or even pullet egg, duck egg, or hen's egg. People also used items they had in their homes for measuring. Recipes called for measuring by the wine glass, tumbler, teacup, or coffee cup, as well as salt spoon for small amounts. A recipe would turn out very differently if the cook had a larger hand than the person who wrote the recipe, or if they had a different idea about the size of a hazel nut or whatever comparison was used. It sounds funny to us today to think of cooking with such measurements. It would have been difficult to learn to cook from those recipes.

## Level Standard Measurement

There were some early attempts at making measurements that would be consistent regardless of who the cook was. However, it wasn't until about eighty years ago that recipes became more widely available that listed ingredients by level standard size cups, tablespoons, and teaspoons. Then it became possible to predict the success of a recipe by always measuring ingredients the same way. Flour had to be sifted and lightly piled into a measuring cup until it was overflowing. Then the flour was leveled off with a straight edge of a knife to get an exact measure. Although this was a somewhat more difficult method, it was obviously more accurate than measuring by the handful or by comparisons with eggs, nuts, etc.

## Metric Measurement

The metric system is a decimal system based upon a standard length, the meter. Although to us the metric system seems new, it was actually developed over one hundred and eighty-five years ago. (Changes have been made as science and technology progressed and more accuracy was needed.) The United States is the last large country to change to the metric system. Trade with other countries has made it important for us to have a system of measurement which agrees with that used by the rest of the industrial nations of the world.

As we begin to use metric units in measuring all sorts of things, including the food we buy, it's time to begin using metric measurements in cooking. You will be glad to know that the metric system is a simple and logical one. There is no need for fractions, since smaller numbers are based on units of 10, or the decimal, just as our dollar is divided into tens and hundreds. In cooking we will carry the decimal system just one step further and measure in thousands of a metric unit. We need to learn only a few new terms. Where we used to measure volume of an ingredient in quarts, cups, tablespoons, and teaspoons, we will now be measuring in terms of the *liter* (abbreviated *L*) and *milliliter (mL)*. There are 1,000 milliliters in a liter. The unit of measure we will use more often in cooking is the *milliliter*. When we measure liquid or dry ingredients by volume, we will find that a recipe calls for a certain number of milliliters.

If we wish to weigh something, instead of using ounces and pounds, we will measure in terms of *kilograms* (abbreviated *kg*) and *grams (g)*. There are 1,000 grams in a kilogram. The *gram* is the unit of measure we will use more often in cooking. If we weigh dry ingredients, we will see that a recipe calls for a certain number of grams.

# Metric Measurement by Volume

The technique of measuring ingredients by volume is the same as it has been ever since measurement by the level standard cup was established about eighty years ago. The only differences in measuring by *metric* volume are the size of the container used and the size and name of the unit being measured.

There are only two terms you need to know for measuring by volume—*liter* (abbreviated *L*) and *milliliter (mL)*. There are 1,000 milliliters in a liter. The *milliliter* is the unit of measure we will use more often in cooking.

## *Equipment You Will Need*

1. To measure dry ingredients by volume, you need a dry measuring set marked in milliliters. This dry measuring set is a set of three containers marked 50 mL, 125 mL, and 250 mL.

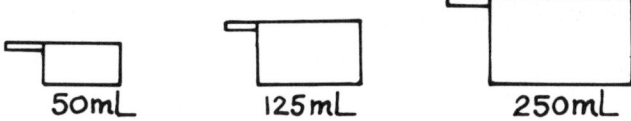

2. In order to measure small amounts of ingredients such as baking soda, vanilla, etc., you will need a set of metric measuring spoons. The spoons are marked 1 mL, 2 mL, 5 mL, 15 mL, and 25 mL.

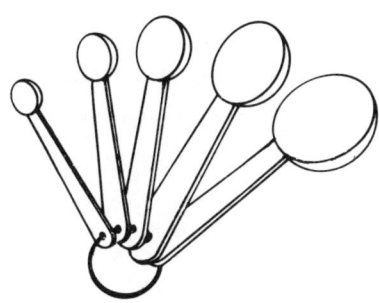

3. For measuring liquids, a clear measure marked in milliliters is needed. It should be clear so you can see the level of the liquid being measured.

## *How to Use Metric Dry-Measure Containers*

When a recipe calls for 50 mL, 125 mL, or 250 mL, it will be easy to measure in the right container because the set is marked that way. But if the recipe calls for 375 mL, you would use the 250-mL container and the 125-mL container to equal 375 mL.

$$250\,mL + 125\,mL = 375\,mL$$

If it calls for 500 mL, you would fill the 250-mL container twice.

$$250\,mL + 250\,mL = 500\,mL$$

If it called for 175 mL, you would use the 125-mL container and the 50-mL container to equal 175 mL.

$$125\,mL + 50\,mL = 175\,mL$$

The 25-mL measuring spoon should be used when that much extra is needed. For example, to measure 150 mL, you would use the 125-mL container and the 25-mL measuring spoon.

## *How to Measure Dry Ingredients by Volume*

1. *Flour* has a tendency to pack down and needs to be made lighter by sifting or by stirring it with a spoon in order to get a measurement that is always the same. Lightly fill the measuring container to overflowing. Use the straight edge of a knife or spatula and scrape off the excess for a full measure.

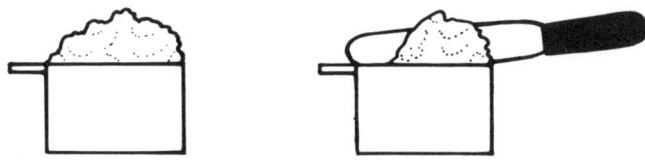

2. *Brown sugar* should be packed into the container. If the brown sugar has been properly packed into the container, it retains its shape when emptied from the container.
3. *Granulated sugar and other dry ingredients* are put into the container to overflowing and leveled off with a straight edge of a knife or spatula.
4. *Fat* is packed into the container so that there are no trapped air spaces, and then leveled off with a knife to have a full measure. Look for margarine and butter wrappers that are marked to show milliliters; this will make it easier to measure sticks of margarine or butter.
5. *Small amounts* of dry ingredients are measured by filling a

metric measuring spoon to overflowing and then leveling it off with the straight edge of a knife.

## How to Measure Liquids

Measure all liquids in a clear measure marked in milliliters (abbreviated *mL*), so you can see the level of the liquid.

Put the measure on a table or other level surface to read the amount correctly. (If you hold the measure, it can easily tip and there might appear to be either more or less liquid than it actually contains.) Check the amount of liquid by bending down so your eye is on the same level as the liquid.

Often the amount of liquid called for in a recipe is not one of the numbers printed on the clear liquid measure. Since we are measuring in milliliters, it is easy to adjust for a recipe that calls for a little more or a little less liquid than the amounts marked on the liquid measure. Just imagine that there are lines between the numbers. In the drawing below the imaginary or dotted lines indicate 210, 220, 230, and 240 mL.

```
-250-
- - - - - -
- - - - - -
- - - - - -
- - - - - -
-200-
```

If a recipe calls for 240 mL, fill the liquid up to a little less than 250 mL.

You can see the level to which it must be filled for 60 mL or 120 mL.

Small amounts of liquid ingredients, such as vanilla, are measured with a metric measuring spoon. The metric measuring spoons are marked 1 mL, 2 mL, 5 mL, 15 mL, and 25 mL.

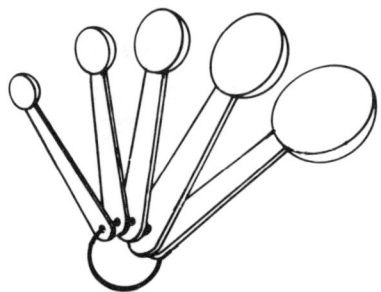

## Metric Measurement by Mass (Weight)

Measurement by mass (weight) is another way to measure dry ingredients. They can be weighed on a scale. It is a shortcut in measuring, since you can just pour out the amount the recipe calls for rather than measuring in several containers.

There are only two terms you will need to know—*kilogram* (abbreviated *kg*) and *gram* (*g*). There are 1,000 grams in a kilogram. The *gram* is the unit of measure we will use more often in cooking.

## *Equipment You Will Need*
1. You will need a scale marked in grams. If you are buying a scale, a kitchen scale will have advantages over a small diet scale; however, if you already have a diet scale on hand, it could be used.

2. If the scale does not have a bowl, you will need a plastic or other lightweight container for holding things to be weighed.

Even though you are going to measure dry ingredients by mass (weight), you will need to measure small amounts of ingredients by volume. You will need the measuring spoons mentioned in the previous section on measurement by volume in order to measure salt, baking powder, etc. Of course, you will have to measure liquid ingredients by volume using the clear liquid measure marked in milliliters.

## *Get Acquainted with Your Scale*

You will notice that the scale is marked off in units of 100 g, 200 g, etc.

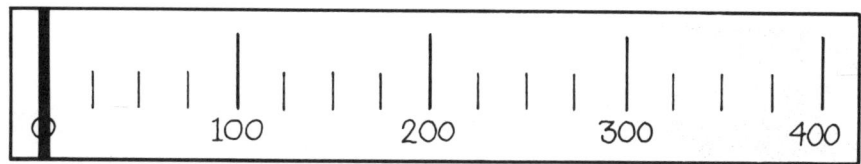

The scale may also be marked in ounces, but for the recipes in this book, use the metric scale. Count the lines between 100-gram markings. If the scale has three lines, each mark equals 25 grams.

OR

The scale may have four lines between the 100-gram markings. If so, each mark equals 20 grams.

OR

The scale may have ten lines between the 100-gram markings. Each mark equals 10 grams, and the large mark points out 50 grams.

OR

Your scale may be marked in a different way. Study the scale so that you will know how to read your scale.

Do you see the indicator that shows the weight?

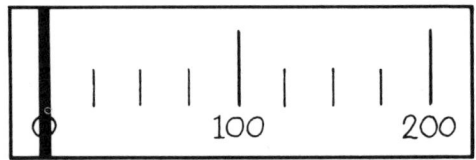

Find the knob for setting the indicator to 0.

## How to Use the Scale

Put the lightweight bowl on the scale.

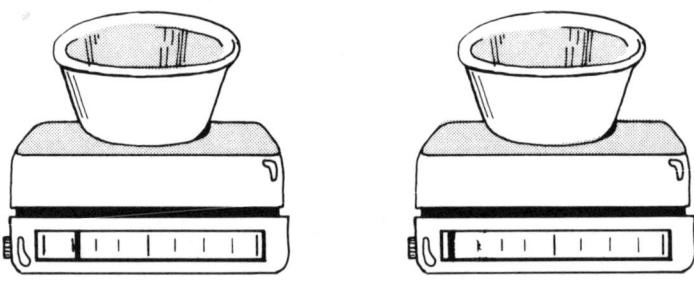

Set the indicator to 0. *Always* start in this way, with the indicator at 0, so that the scale shows only the weight of the ingredient in the bowl. (Otherwise, part of the weight shown would be the weight of the bowl.)

All solid or dry ingredients (such as flour, sugar, fat) can be weighed on the scale. Just add the ingredient until the indicator shows the number of grams needed. Empty the bowl before weighing the next ingredient. Then you won't get confused by trying to add each new amount to the previous weight.

## Metric Measurement of Pan Sizes

Use a metric ruler in measuring the size of the pans. The ruler is marked in *centimeters* (abbreviated *cm*). Measure across the top of the pan to find the dimensions listed for the pan. Most of the pan sizes called for in the recipes are probably already in your kitchen (since they are the usual sizes), but we are measuring them in centimeters instead of inches. Two of the nut breads given in this book are baked in small loaf pans. Small, inexpensive aluminum-foil pans, about 9 cm by 15 cm, work very nicely and are re-usable.

## Metric Measurement of Baking Temperature

There is another metric term used in the recipes, and that is *degrees Celsius* (abbreviated °C). The baking temperatures are also listed in degrees Fahrenheit (° F) because that is the way our oven-temperature scales are measured now. The degrees Celsius are listed because someday the oven temperature scales will be changed, and it is a good idea to begin thinking in metric units now.

## Non-Metric Terms

The following non-metric cooking terms may need defining. A *pinch* is the amount of ingredient that can be held between the tip of the index finger and the thumb. A *dash* is one shake of an ingredient from a shaker.

## Let's Develop Good Work Habits

When you're beginning to learn how to do something, if you start out doing it correctly, it soon becomes a habit that you don't have to think about. (When you learned to tie a shoe, at first you had to carefully remember how to hold and turn the shoe lace, before it became such an easy part of dressing.) So let's begin by developing good work habits in the kitchen.

1. Start out by getting *yourself* ready to cook. If you have long hair that might get in your way or get in the food you are preparing, tie it back neatly; protect your clothes from spills by putting on an apron; then wash your hands.

2. Read the entire recipe carefully.

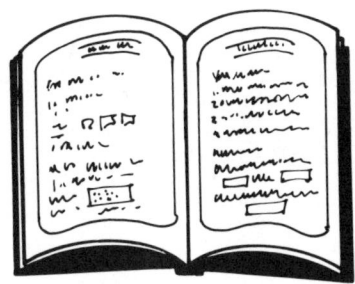

3. Organize the bowls, spoons, pans, and other equipment that you will need.
4. Put out all the ingredients for the recipe.
5. Measure ingredients accurately.

6. Follow the recipe in mixing the ingredients.
7. Check the recipe to see if anything was forgotten. If you did forget something, it usually isn't too late to add it.
8. Then bake or finish cooking the product.
9. While the product is cooking, put things away and clean up the kitchen.
10. Stay in the kitchen while things are baking; if you forget them, they will bake too long or burn.

## How to Tell When Baking Is Done

Every beginner needs help in knowing when cookies, bread, or cake have baked long enough. Here are some guides. It is good to use two of these tests so you will feel more confident in knowing when the food is done.

## For Cookies
Place the oven racks near the center of the oven.

1. If the baking temperature is right, the *color* can be a good indication that cookies are done. A beautiful golden brown color probably means they are done, just the way you like them. Just be careful not to get the bottom of the cookies too dark.
2. They will also feel firm if touched lightly with a finger; if your finger leaves an indentation, they need to be baked longer.

NOT DONE    DONE

## For Brownies, Bread, or Cake Baked in Pans
If you are baking them in a *glass* pan, lower the temperature of the oven 25° F. For example, if the recipe says 350° F, bake at 325° F.

1. The baked product will shrink away from the sides of the pan somewhat when it is done.

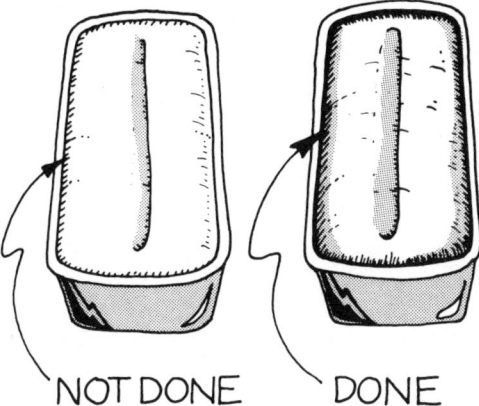

2. It will feel firm if touched lightly with a finger.
3. Insert a toothpick into the center of the baked product. If it is done, no batter or crumbs should cling to the toothpick.

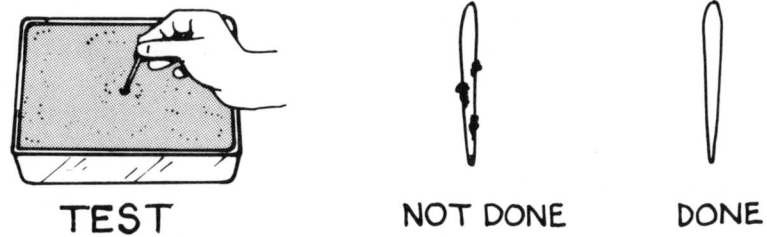

You may find that things bake more quickly or slowly in your oven than the recipes suggest. Some ovens are not accurate, so you may need to adjust the baking temperature accordingly. If you find cookies, bread, etc., are getting too dark in the suggested baking time, lower the baking temperature 25° F. (For example, if the recipe says 350° F, bake at 325° F.) On the other hand, if you find your oven takes much longer to bake a product than the recipe suggests, raise the baking temperature 25° F. (For example, if the recipe says 350° F, bake at 375° F.)

## Recipes Let You Choose Your Method of Measuring

Dry ingredients given in the recipes in this book are listed so they can be measured either by volume, in milliliters, or by mass (weight), in grams. You can choose the method you use for measuring. As a helpful reminder, this symbol of a standard measuring container  appears above items listed in the column to be measured by volume, and this symbol of a scale  appears above items listed in the column of dry ingredients to be measured by mass (weight).

*For example:*

500 mL flour                OR   240 g flour
10 mL baking powder
5 mL salt
30 mL sugar

You would measure 500 mL flour by volume in metric dry-measure containers *or* weigh 240 g flour on the scale. The next three ingredients, which are small amounts, should be measured by volume (not weighed) in metric measuring spoons.

The recipes in this book have been tested for measuring both by volume and by mass (weight). The proportions have been adjusted so they can be measured conveniently in the metric dry-measure containers. It should not be assumed that a given volume of an ingredient is exactly equal to the mass (weight) of the ingredient given in the recipe.

## *Packaged Foods*
Some of the recipes call for packages of various items, such as chocolate chips, frozen fruits, and vegetables. The food companies have marked standard-sized packages with the exact conversion of the ounces into grams, and so they may have odd-sounding amounts, such as 183 grams. The packages are standard sizes so don't worry about looking for the exact amount given in the recipe—a close approximation will do.

Many of the recipes call for margarine. Soft margarine is easier to mix, even when cold, than margarine sold in sticks. However, those margarines labeled as "whipped", "spread," or "diet" are not appropriate for baking. They have a high content of water or so much air whipped into them that they do not have enough shortening to give the results you want.

# RECIPES

Along with learning how to measure ingredients and follow a recipe, I hope beginning cooks will discover the enormous pleasure in successfully making delicious food. If you have a sense of curiosity, you will see the beauty of a meringue, enjoy the feel of kneading a biscuit dough, taste new flavor combinations in the quick breads, smell the aroma of baking cookies, and in general find the pleasure of cooking that experience will bring.

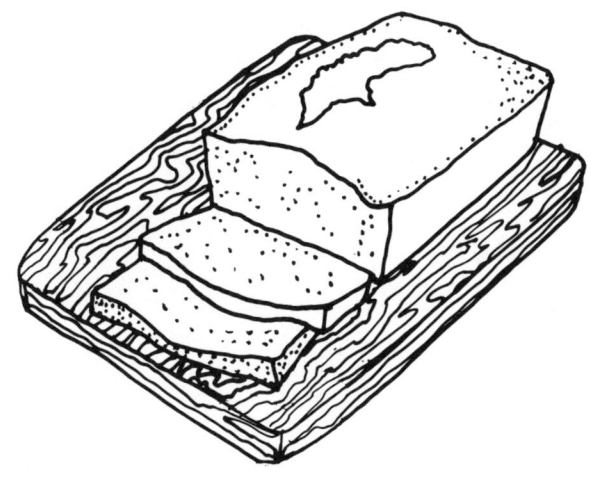

# BROWNIES AND COOKIES

Cookie and brownie recipes are a good starting point for the beginning cook. By measuring accurately and following the directions of the recipes you will have something delicious to eat before long.

# BROWNIES

Brownies are easy to make and are always popular.

1. Light oven and set it to 350° F (180° C).
2. In a saucepan, melt over low heat:

    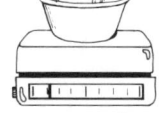

      100 mL margarine     OR    75 g margarine
      2 squares baking chocolate
   Stir occasionally to prevent the chocolate from sticking. Then take pan off the heat.
3. Add and stir until blended:
      300 mL sugar                OR    250 g sugar
4. Add and stir until mixed well:
      2 eggs
      5 mL vanilla
5. Mix together:
      250 mL flour                 OR    120 g flour
      2 mL baking powder
      2 mL salt
   Add to the other ingredients and stir until mixed well.
6. Grease 20-cm square pan and put the brownie batter into the pan.
7. *Bake for 30 minutes.* Remember the pan is *hot*, so use a pot holder. Test to see if it is done by putting a toothpick into the center of the brownies. If no crumbs cling to the toothpick when it is taken out, the brownies are done.

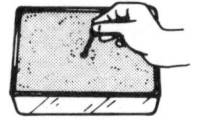
TEST

NOT DONE    DONE

*Recipe continued on next page.*

**8.** Cool the brownies 10 minutes and then cut into squares and remove from pan.

*Recipe Makes:* 25 brownies

## BUTTERSCOTCH BROWNIES

These are a chewy variation on the usual brownie recipe.

1. Light oven and set it to 350° F (180° C).
2. Melt in a saucepan over low heat:

      125 mL margarine         OR   110 g margarine
   Remove the pan from the heat.
3. Add and mix well:
      300 mL light brown sugar   OR  300 g light brown sugar

      7 mL vanilla
4. Add and mix well:
   2 eggs
5. Mix together:
      375 mL flour           OR   180 g flour
      5 mL baking powder
   Then add to other ingredients and mix well.
6. Stir in:
      250 mL chopped walnuts   OR  120 g chopped walnuts

7. Grease 20-cm square baking pan.
8. Put the brownie batter into the pan.
9. *Bake 35 to 45 minutes.* Remember the pan is *hot,* so use a pot holder. Brownies will feel firm to a light touch when done, or a toothpick put in the center of the brownies will come out without any batter clinging to it.

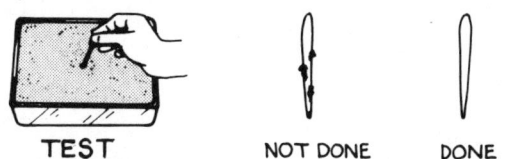

TEST   NOT DONE   DONE

10. Cool 10 minutes before cutting into squares. Remove cut brownies from pan.

*Recipe Makes: 25 brownies*

## CHOCOLATE-CHIP COOKIES

These are always a hit with anyone who likes chocolate.

1. Light oven and set it to 350° F (180° C).
2. In a mixing bowl, stir together thoroughly, using a wooden spoon:

| 250 mL margarine | OR | 220 g margarine |
| 175 mL light brown sugar | OR | 150 g light brown sugar |
| 175 mL granulated sugar | OR | 150 g granulated sugar |

3. Add and stir well:
   5 mL vanilla
   2 eggs

4. Mix together:
   550 mL flour           OR   270 g flour
   5 mL baking soda
   2 mL salt
   Add gradually to other ingredients and mix well.

5. Add and stir into cookie mixture:
   1 package chocolate chips (170 g)

6. Drop by teaspoonful (about 15 mL) onto ungreased cookie sheet. Leave space of about 4 cm between the cookies so

they won't run into each other while they bake. You can put two cookie sheets in the oven to bake at one time.

7. *Bake 8 to 10 minutes.* Remember the cookie sheet is *hot*, so use a pot holder. The cookies should be beautifully browned and firm to the touch when they are done.

8. Remove the baked cookies form the cookie sheet with a pancake turner.
9. Before putting another batch of cookies on the cookie sheet, scrape off any bits of cookie crumbs and wipe the cookie sheet with a paper towel.

*Recipe Makes:* 96 cookies

# CHOCOLATE-CHIP MERINGUE COOKIES

This is a light, crisp cookie that is nice for parties and special occasions.

1. Light oven and set it to 300° F (150° C).
2. Separate the egg whites from the yolks by cracking the shell and moving the yolk from one half of the shell to the other while the white drains into a bowl. Don't get any yolk into the whites, as they will not beat well. (Refrigerate yolks with a small amount of water in a covered container for another use.)
   Separate and put into a mixing bowl:
     4 egg whites
3. Add to egg whites in bowl and beat with an egg-beater or electric mixer until stiff:
     1 mL cream of tartar
     pinch of salt
4. Add gradually and continue beating until stiff:

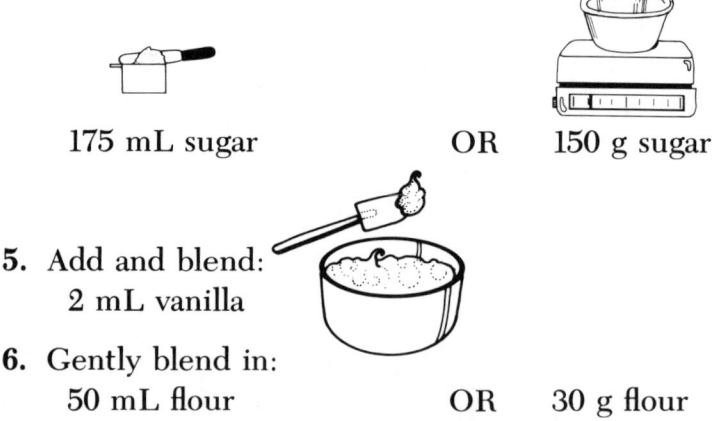

   175 mL sugar          OR     150 g sugar

5. Add and blend:
     2 mL vanilla
6. Gently blend in:
     50 mL flour           OR     30 g flour

7. Gently blend in:
    1 package chocolate chips (170 g)
    125 mL chopped walnuts     OR   60 g chopped walnuts

8. Cut pieces of paper (grocery bags will do) to fit the cookie sheets.

9. Drop by teaspoonful onto the paper covering the cookie sheet. You can put two cookie sheets in the oven at one time.
10. *Bake 25 minutes.* Remember the cookie sheet is *hot,* so use a pot holder. The cookies will be lightly browned, dry, and firm to the touch when they are done.
11. Use a table knife to remove the cookies from the paper to cool.

*Recipe Makes:* **44 cookies**

# DATE BARS

These have a sweet layer of dates between thick layers of dough that have a nice texture.

1. Light oven and set it to 350° F (180° C).
2. Cut into pieces and put into a saucepan:

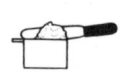     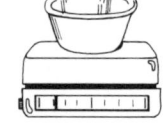

    250 mL dates             OR   180 g dates

3. Add to dates and boil gently until mixture is as thick as jam:

    250 mL water
    125 mL sugar            OR   100 g sugar

Do not undercook this. It will take 10 to 15 minutes. Stir to prevent it from sticking.

4. In a mixing bowl, stir together thoroughly, using a wooden spoon:

    175 mL margarine        OR   165 g margarine
    300 mL light brown sugar   OR   265 g light brown sugar

    2 mL vanilla

5. Mix together:

    250 mL dry oatmeal       OR   110 g dry oatmeal
    375 mL flour               OR   180 g flour
    2 mL baking soda

Add to the sugar and margarine and mix well.

6. Put 2/3 of the dough into a greased 20-cm square baking pan. Use your hand to press it into the corners and pat it flat.

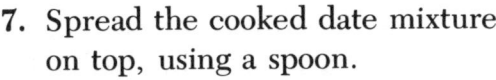

7. Spread the cooked date mixture on top, using a spoon.

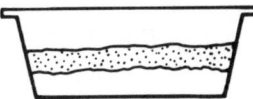

8. Top with the remaining cookie dough and pat it flat with your hand.

9. *Bake 35 to 40 minutes.* Remember the pan is *hot,* so use a pot holder. The top should be brown all over when done.
10. Cool 10 minutes and then cut into square pieces and remove from pan.

*Recipe Makes:* 25 date bars.

# DATE-NUT MERINGUE COOKIES

This is a wonderful light cookie for parties and special occasions.

1. Light oven and set it to 300° F (150° C).
2. Separate the egg whites from the yolks by cracking the shell and moving the yolk from one half of the shell to the other while the white drains into a bowl. Don't get any yolk into the whites as they will not beat well. (Refrigerate yolks with a small amount of water in a covered container for another use.)
   Separate and put into a mixing bowl:
      4 egg whites
3. Add to egg whites in bowl and beat with an egg-beater or electric mixer until stiff:
      1 mL cream of tartar
      pinch of salt
4. Add gradually and continue beating until stiff:

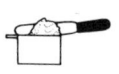   

   175 mL sugar         OR   150 g sugar

5. Add and blend:
      2 mL vanilla
6. Gently blend in:
      50 mL flour        OR   40 g flour
7. Gently blend in:
      125 mL dates, cut up    OR   90 g dates, cut up
      125 mL chopped walnuts  OR   60 g chopped walnuts

8. Cut pieces of paper (grocery bags will do) to fit the cookie sheets.

9. Drop by teaspoonful onto the paper covering the cookie sheet. You can put two cookie sheets in the oven at one time.
10. *Bake 25 minutes.* Remember the cookie sheet is *hot,* so use a pot holder. The cookies will be lightly browned, dry, and firm to the touch when they are done.
11. Use a table knife to remove the cookies from the paper to cool.

*Recipe Makes:* 44 cookies.

# GINGER COOKIES

These crispy, spicy cookies are especially good with milk, baked custard, or anything mild.

1. Light oven and set it to 350° F (180° C).
2. Put in a mixing bowl and stir thoroughly with a wooden spoon:

   | 200 mL margarine | OR | 165 g margarine |
   | 250 mL sugar | OR | 200 g sugar |

3. Add and stir well:
   1 egg
   50 mL molasses         OR      80 g molasses

4. Mix together:
   625 mL flour           OR      300 g flour
   10 mL baking soda
   1 mL salt
   2 mL ginger
   5 mL cinnamon

   Add gradually to the other ingredients and stir well.

5. Drop by teaspoonful onto ungreased cookie sheet. Leave space of about 4 cm on the cookie sheet between the cookies so they won't run into each other while they bake. You can put two cookie sheets in the oven to bake at one time.

6. *Bake 8 to 10 minutes.* Remember the cookie sheet is *hot*, so use a pot holder. When they are done, the cookies should feel firm when touched lightly with the finger.
7. Remove the baked cookies from the cookie sheet with a pancake turner.
8. Before putting a second batch of cookies on the cookie sheet, scrape off any bits of cookie and wipe the cookie sheet with a paper towel.

*Recipe Makes:* 55 cookies

## PEANUT-BUTTER COOKIES

"Try these, they're great."
1. Light oven and set it to 350° F (180° C).
2. Mix together thoroughly in a bowl, using a wooden spoon:

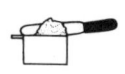 

| | | |
|---|---|---|
| 125 mL light brown sugar | OR | 100 g light brown sugar |
| 125 mL granulated sugar | OR | 100 g granulated sugar |
| 125 mL margarine | OR | 110 g margarine |

3. Add and mix well:
   2 mL vanilla
   1 egg
   250 mL peanut butter          OR   250 g peanut butter

*Recipe continued on next page.*

4. Mix together:
   375 mL flour          OR     180 g flour
   2 mL salt
   2 mL baking soda
   Add to the other ingredients and mix well.
5. Drop by teaspoonful onto ungreased cookie sheet.
6. Dip a fork in flour and then flatten each cookie with a cross-hatched design made by the tines of the fork. You can put two cookie sheets in the oven at one time.

7. *Bake 8 to 10 minutes.* Remember the cookie sheet is *hot*, so use a pot holder. When they are done, the cookies should be brown and firm when touched lightly with a finger.
8. Remove the baked cookies from the cookie sheet with a pancake turner.
9. Before putting another batch of cookies on the cookie sheet, scrape off any bits of cookie and wipe the cookie sheet with a paper towel.

*Recipe Makes:* **67 cookies**

# REFRIGERATOR DATE PINWHEELS

These taste as good as they look!

## *Filling*
1. Put in a saucepan and cook over low heat until mixture is as thick as jam (about 10 to 15 minutes):

    550 mL chopped dates    OR    400 g chopped dates
    250 mL sugar    OR    200 g sugar
    250 mL water
  Stir to prevent it from sticking.
2. Cool date mixture, then add:
    250 mL chopped walnuts    OR    120 g chopped walnuts

## *Dough*
1. In a mixing bowl, stir together thoroughly with a wooden spoon:
    250 mL margarine    OR    220 g margarine
    425 mL light brown sugar    OR    400 g light brown sugar
2. Add and stir well:
    5 mL vanilla
    3 eggs

*Recipe continued on next page.*

3. Mix together:
   1000 mL flour         OR        540 g flour
   3 mL salt
   2 mL baking soda
   Add gradually to margarine, sugar, and egg mixture. Mix well.
4. Chill dough in refrigerator overnight.
5. After dough is chilled, divide it into two parts and roll out each one separately into a rectangle 20 cm by 26 cm, 1 cm thick.

6. Spread each section of dough with the filling. Then roll up as for a jelly roll.

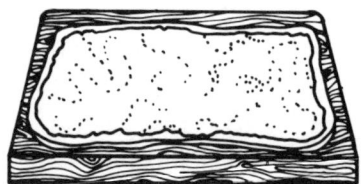 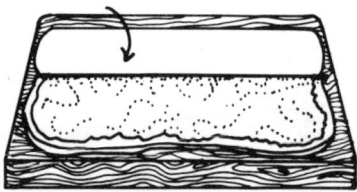

7. Wrap in waxed paper or plastic wrap and chill overnight.

## Baking

1. Light oven and set it to 350° F (180° C).
2. Slice rolls of cookies into 1-cm slices. Place on ungreased cookie sheet. Leave space of about 4 cm between cookies so they won't run into each other while they bake. You can put two cookie sheets in the oven to bake at one time.

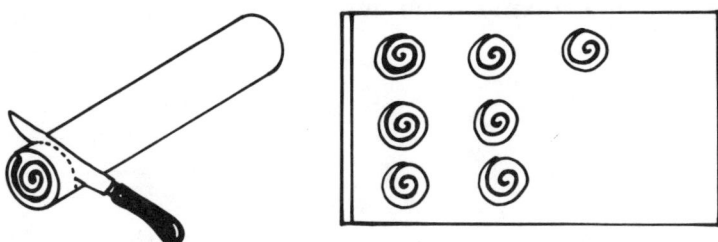

3. *Bake 10 to 12 minutes.* Remember the cookie sheet is *hot*, so use a pot holder. They will be brown and firm to the touch when they are done.
4. Remove the baked cookies from the cookie sheet with a pancake turner.
5. Before putting another batch of cookies on the cookie sheet, scrape off any bits of cookie and wipe the cookie sheet with a paper towel.

*Recipe Makes:* 90 large cookies

# REFRIGERATOR OATMEAL COOKIES

The oatmeal gives these cookies a wonderfully crunchy texture.

1. Put in a mixing bowl and stir thoroughly with a wooden spoon:

   | | | |
   |---|---|---|
   | 125 mL granulated sugar | OR | 100 g granulated sugar |
   | 125 mL light brown sugar | OR | 100 g light brown sugar |
   | 125 mL margarine | OR | 110 g margarine |

2. Add and mix well:
   2 mL vanilla
   1 egg
   25 mL molasses       OR   30 g molasses

3. Mix together:
   200 mL flour              OR   100 g flour
   375 mL dry oatmeal        OR   150 g dry oatmeal
   2 mL baking soda
   2 mL salt
   Gradually add to other ingredients and mix well.

4. Shape into two rolls about 5 cm thick and wrap in waxed paper or plastic wrap. Chill overnight in refrigerator.

## Baking

1. Light oven and set it to 350° F (180° C).
2. Slice chilled cookie dough about 1 cm thick.
3. Place sliced dough on ungreased cookie sheet. Leave space of about 4 cm between cookies. You can put two cookie sheets in the oven at one time.
4. *Bake 8 to 10 minutes.* Remember the cookie sheet is *hot*, so use a pot holder. The cookies will be evenly browned and firm to the touch when they are done.

NOT DONE    DONE

*Recipe Makes:* 55 cookies

# ROLLED SUGAR COOKIES

These make nice Christmas cookies and can be rolled out without being refrigerated first.

1. Light oven and set it to 350° F (180° C).
2. Put in a mixing bowl and stir together thoroughly with a wooden spoon:

   250 mL margarine     OR     220 g margarine
   250 mL sugar     OR     200 g sugar

3. Add and stir well:
   5 mL vanilla
   2 eggs
   15 mL milk

4. Mix together:
   875 mL flour     OR     420 g flour
   1 mL salt
   2 mL baking soda
   Add to the other ingredients and stir well.

5. Flour a bread board and rolling pin with about 25 mL flour. Put half the dough on the board and pat with flour. Roll the dough out until it is .5 cm thick. Roll lightly, to

prevent the dough from sticking to the board and rolling pin. Add a little more flour if it is needed to prevent the dough from sticking.
6. Cut out fancy cookie shapes. Cut them out close together, to make as many cookies as possible.

7. Put the cut-out cookies on ungreased cookie sheets and decorate with colored sugar.
   You can put two cookie sheets in the oven at one time.
8. *Bake 8 to 10 minutes.* Remember the cookie sheets are *hot,* so use a pot holder. The cookies will be lightly browned on the edges when they're done.
9. Remove the baked cookies with a pancake turner.
10. Before putting another batch of cookies on the cookie sheet, scrape off any bits of cookie and sugar, then wipe the cookie sheet with a paper towel.

*Recipe Makes:* 72 cookies, approximately 5 cm in size

## SESAME COOKIES

Sesame seeds and coconut give these cookies a nice texture and flavor.

1. Light oven and set it to 350° F (180° C).
2. Put in a pie pan and bake until lightly brown:

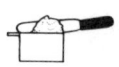   

    125 mL grated coconut    OR   40 g grated coconut
    125 mL sesame seeds    OR   70 g package sesame seeds

   Stir them every few minutes so they brown evenly. Remember the pan is *hot,* so use a pot holder.

3. Mix together thoroughly in a bowl using a wooden spoon:
   200 mL margarine    OR   165 g margarine
   250 mL light brown sugar    OR   200 g light brown sugar
   5 mL vanilla

4. Add and beat well:
   1 egg

5. Add the lightly browned sesame seeds and coconut, and mix well.

6. Stir together and then add:
   500 mL flour    OR   240 g flour
   5 mL baking powder
   5 mL baking soda
   2 mL salt
   Stir well.

7. Shape the dough into balls, using a 5 mL spoon.
8. Place on ungreased cookie sheet and flatten with a fork dipped in flour. You can put two cookie sheets in the oven to bake at one time.

9. *Bake 8 to 10 minutes.* Remember the cookie sheet is *hot,* so use a pot holder. The cookies will be beautifully browned when they're done.
10. Remove the baked cookies from cookie sheet with a pancake turner.
11. Before putting another batch of cookies on the cookie sheet, scrape off any bits of cookie and wipe the cookie sheet with a paper towel.

*Recipe Makes:* 79 cookies

# SOFT SUGAR COOKIES

This is my grandmother's recipe in metric measure. My mother's cookie jar was always filled with these cookies.

1. Light oven and set it to 350° F (180° C).
2. Put in a mixing bowl and stir together thoroughly, using a wooden spoon:

      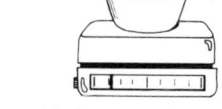

   200 mL margarine   OR   165 g margarine
   250 mL sugar   OR   200 g sugar

3. Add and stir well:
   5 mL vanilla
   2 eggs

4. Add and stir
   160 mL buttermilk

5. Mix together:
   625 mL flour   OR   300 g flour
   2 mL salt
   3 mL baking soda
   5 mL nutmeg

   Add to other ingredients and mix well.

6. Drop by teaspoonful onto ungreased cookie sheet. Leave space of about 4 cm between the cookies so they won't run into each other while they bake.

7. Sprinkle sugar on top of cookies. You can put two cookie sheets in the oven to bake at one time.
8. *Bake 8 to 10 minutes.* Remember the cookie sheet is *hot*, so use a pot holder. Cookies will be lightly browned and firm to the touch when they are done.
9. Remove the cookies from the cookie sheet with a pancake turner.
10. Before putting another batch of cookies on the cookie sheet, scrape off any bits of cookie crumbs and wipe the cookie sheet with a paper towel.

*Recipe Makes:* 52 cookies

## QUICK BREADS

These are called quick breads because they can be made in a fairly short length of time, since they have baking powder and baking soda, rather than yeast, to make them rise. Yeast breads take several hours to rise, while quick breads can be baked as soon as they are mixed.

# BANANA BREAD

When bananas are a little too ripe for eating, they are perfect for making this delicious bread.

1. Light oven and set it to 325° F (160° C).
2. Put in a mixing bowl and stir together thoroughly, using a wooden spoon:

   | 250 mL margarine | OR | 220 g margarine |
   | 500 mL sugar | OR | 400 g sugar |

3. Add and mix well:
   4 eggs
   375 mL pecan pieces     OR   175 g pecan pieces
4. Mix together:
   1000 mL flour           OR   480 g flour
   5 mL baking soda
   5 mL baking powder

   Add to other ingredients and stir until batter is mixed well.
5. Mash with a fork in a bowl or large measuring cup until they are almost runny:
   2–3 very ripe bananas (250 mL, mashed)
   Stir bananas into batter until well mixed.
6. Grease 4 loaf pans, 9 cm x 15 cm. Divide the batter evenly into the pans.

*Recipe continued on next page.*

7. *Bake 1½ hours.* Remember the pans are *hot,* so use a pot holder. The bread will be well browned when it is done; you can also test it by putting a toothpick into the center. If no crumbs cling to the toothpick when it is taken out, the bread is done.

NOT DONE    DONE

8. Cool in the pans for 5 minutes and then remove from the pans. Allow to cool completely before slicing.
9. Store in plastic bags.

*Recipe Makes:* 4 small loaves

# BISCUITS

These are flaky and tender, and good with honey.

1. Light oven and set it to 450° F (230° C).
2. Mix together in a bowl:

500 mL flour      OR   240 g flour
10 mL baking powder
5 mL salt

3. Add, and blend by cutting it in with two knives or a pastry blender:

    75 mL hydrogenated fat    OR   60 g hydrogenated fat
    (for example, Crisco)

Blend until the fat is the size of peas. Push the ingredients to the sides of the bowl, making a space in the center for the milk.

4. Add, and stir with a fork until the dry ingredients are well mixed:
    170 mL milk

*Recipe continued on next page.*

5. Flour a bread board and rolling pin with 25 mL flour. Knead the dough by folding it over in the flour about 5 times.

6. Roll out the dough lightly until it is 2 cm thick.

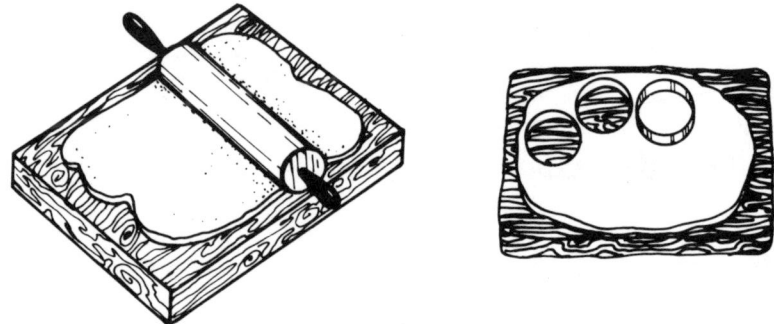

7. Dip a biscuit cutter in flour and use it to cut out the biscuits. Cut them close together to make as many as possible. Shape the remaining dough into round biscuit shapes.
8. Put the biscuits on an ungreased baking sheet.
9. Brush the tops of the biscuits with milk so they will brown nicely.
10. *Bake about 12 minutes.* The biscuits will be lightly browned when done. Remember the baking sheet is *hot,* so use a pot holder.
11. Remove the biscuits from the baking sheet and serve at once.

*Recipe Makes:* 12 biscuits

## BUTTERMILK PANCAKES

These are the thick variety that my family likes best. This recipe can also be used to make good, crisp waffles.

1. Mix in a bowl with an egg beater:
    300 mL buttermilk
    30 mL salad oil
    1 egg

2. Mix together:

    300 mL flour          OR          150 g flour
    15 mL sugar
    2 mL salt
    10 mL baking powder
    2 mL baking soda

Add liquid ingredients and beat with egg-beater until smooth.

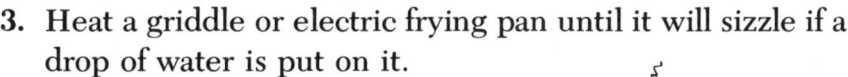

3. Heat a griddle or electric frying pan until it will sizzle if a drop of water is put on it.

*Recipe continued on next page.*

If the griddle is always washed with soap and water (not detergent), it won't have to be greased, and it is easier to clean later; otherwise, brush with oil before baking first batch of pancakes, to prevent sticking.
4. Put 15 mL batter on griddle for each pancake. Leave enough room between pancakes so they can be turned easily.
5. Turn the pancakes when bubbles form on the top of the pancakes, or look at the underside by lifting the edge. If the color is a nice brown, turn them with a pancake turner to brown on the other side. It takes a bit of practice to turn pancakes easily. You'll enjoy learning.
6. Serve at once while they're hot, with syrup.

*Recipe Makes: 32 pancakes*

# COFFEE CAKE

This is a light cake with cinnamon topping, and a nice treat for a leisurely breakfast.

1. Light oven and set it to 375° F (190° C).
2. Mix together in a bowl:

    175 mL sugar             OR     150 g sugar
    75 mL margarine      OR     55 g margarine

3. Mix in:
   1 egg

4. Add and mix well:
   120 mL milk

5. Mix together:
   375 mL flour            OR     180 g flour
   10 mL baking powder
   2 mL salt
   Add to other ingredients and mix well.
7. Grease 20-cm square pan and spread batter in pan.
8. Mix together and spread over batter:
   125 mL light brown sugar    OR    100 g light brown sugar
   7 mL cinnamon

9. *Bake 25 to 30 minutes.* Remember the pan is *hot,* so use a pot holder. Test to see if it is done by putting a toothpick

*Recipe continued on next page.*

into the center. If no crumbs cling to the toothpick when it is taken out, the cake is done.

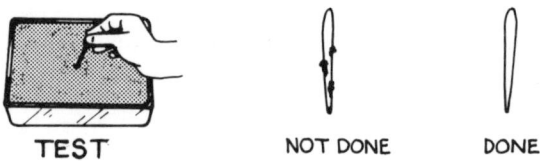

TEST      NOT DONE      DONE

*Recipe Makes:* 1 coffee cake (9 servings)

---

## GRAPENUT BREAD

---

There is no fat in this recipe. One of my children said, "If the bread tastes this good, I'll have to try the cereal."

1. Put in a small bowl and set aside:

    125 mL grapenut cereal   OR  50 g grapenut cereal
    250 mL buttermilk

2. Mix together in a bowl:
   1 egg
   175 mL sugar           OR  150 g sugar

3. Add the grapenut mixture to the egg and sugar mixture.

4. Mix together:
   - 500 mL flour          OR   240 g flour
   - 2 mL baking soda
   - 2 mL salt
   - 5 mL baking powder

   Add to other ingredients and mix well.
5. Grease a bread loaf pan 11 cm x 21 cm.
6. Put batter in pan and let stand for 20 minutes. (This gives more time to soften the grapenuts and add flavor to the bread.)
7. Light oven and set it to 350° F (180° C).
8. *Bake bread 1 hour.* The bread is done when a toothpick inserted in the center of the bread has no batter clinging to it when it is taken out; also, the bread will shrink away from the sides of the pan somewhat.

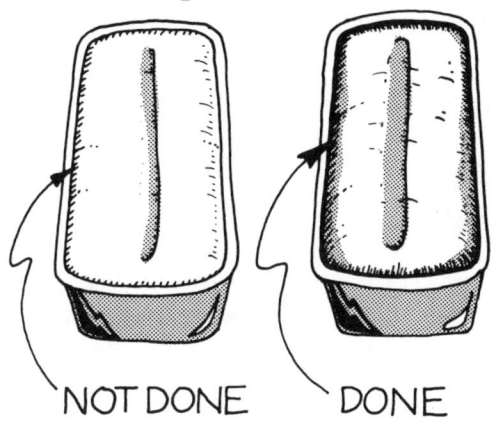

NOT DONE    DONE

9. Cool loaf 10 minutes before removing from pan.
10. After bread has cooled, wrap it in aluminum foil or plastic wrap.

*Recipe Makes:* 1 loaf

# MUFFINS

These muffins can make a simple menu special.

1. Light oven and set it to 425° F (220° C).
2. Mix together in a bowl:

    500 mL flour        OR        240 g flour
    10 mL baking powder
    5 mL salt
    30 mL sugar

   Push mixture to the sides of the bowl, making a space in the center for the liquid ingredients.
3. In another bowl, mix together with an egg-beater:
    1 egg
    250 mL milk
    60 mL salad oil
4. Pour liquid ingredients into the center of the dry ingredients. Stir with a fork until the dry ingredients are dampened. The batter should look lumpy.

5. Grease 12 cups of a muffin pan.
6. With a spoon, carefully put the batter in the muffin cups. Stir the batter as little as possible.
7. *Bake 18 to 20 minutes.* Remember the pans are *hot,* so use a pot holder. The muffins will be beautifully browned and will have shrunk a little away from the sides of the pan when they are done.
8. Remove the muffins from the pan by turning it upside down and tapping it on the table.

9. Serve at once.

   *Recipe Makes:* 12 muffins

# BLUEBERRY MUFFINS

These are filled with lots of blueberries.

1. Light oven and set it to 425° F (220° C).
2. Mix together in a bowl:

        OR

   500 mL flour                    240 g flour
   10 mL baking powder
   5 mL salt
   30 mL sugar

   Push mixture to the sides of the bowl making a space in the center for the liquid ingredients.
3. In another bowl, mix together with an egg-beater:
   1 egg
   250 mL milk
   60 mL salad oil
4. Wash:
   250 mL fresh blueberries
   OR
   Wash canned blueberries in a strainer under cold running water and drain:
   125 mL canned blueberries
   OR
   Use, while they are still frozen:
   250 mL frozen blueberries
5. Pour the liquid ingredients from step 3 into the dry ingre-

dients from step 2. Stir with a fork until the dry ingredients are dampened. The batter should look lumpy.

6. Carefully stir the blueberries into the batter so the fruit isn't crushed and the batter isn't overmixed.
7. Grease 16 cups of muffin pans.
8. With a spoon, carefully put the batter in the muffin cups. Stir the batter as little as possible.
9. *Bake 18 to 20 minutes.* Remember the pans are *hot,* so use a pot holder. The muffins will be beautifully browned and will have shrunk a little away from the sides of the pan when they are done.
10. Remove the muffins from the pan by turning it upside down and tapping it on the table.
11. Serve at once.

*Recipe Makes:* 16 muffins

# CRANBERRY MUFFINS

This is a nice variation when cranberries are in season.

1. Light oven and set it to 425° F (220° C).
2. Mix together in a bowl:

   500 mL flour        OR        240 g flour
   10 mL baking powder
   5 mL salt
   30 mL sugar

   Push mixture to the sides of the bowl, making a space in the center for the liquid ingredients.
3. In another bowl, mix together with an egg-beater:
   1 egg
   250 mL milk
   60 mL salad oil
4. Wash, cut in half, and put in a bowl:
   125 mL fresh cranberries
5. Mix cranberries with:
   30 mL sugar
6. Pour the liquid ingredients from step 3 into the dry ingre-

dients from step 2. Stir with a fork until the dry ingredients are dampened. The batter should look lumpy.
7. Stir the cranberries and sugar into the batter. Don't overmix the batter.
8. Grease 16 cups of muffin pans.
9. With a spoon, carefully put the batter in the muffin cups. Stir the batter as little as possible.
10. *Bake 18 to 20 minutes.* Remember the pans are *hot,* so use a pot holder. The muffins will be beautifully browned and will have shrunk a little away from the sides of the pan when they are done.
11. Remove the muffins from the pan by turning it upside down and tapping it on the table.
12. Serve at once.

*Recipe Makes:* 16 muffins.

# POPOVERS

Popovers are so easy to make and such fun to eat. The oven needs to be very hot, so don't peek into the oven until the last 10 minutes of baking.

1. Light oven and set it to 425° F (220° C).
2. Put cookie sheet on rack in middle of oven.

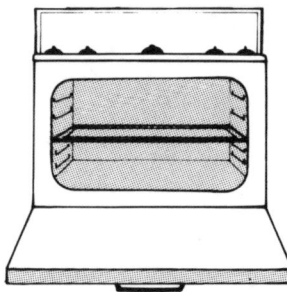

3. Grease generously 6 glass baking cups. The non-stick sprays work even better than greasing the cups.
4. Beat together in a bowl with a beater, or blend in a blender:

2 eggs
250 mL milk
250 mL flour          OR     120 g flour
2 mL salt

5. Fill baking cups ¾ full.

6. Put them in the oven on the hot cookie sheet and *bake 35 to 40 minutes.* The popovers will have "popped over" the edge of the cups and browned beautifully when they are done.

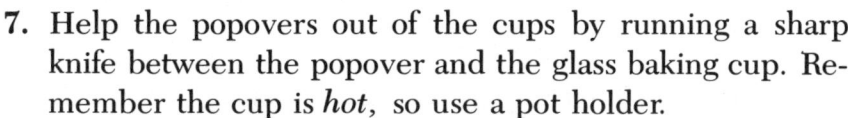

7. Help the popovers out of the cups by running a sharp knife between the popover and the glass baking cup. Remember the cup is *hot,* so use a pot holder.
8. Serve at once.

    *Recipe Makes:* 5 to 6 popovers

## WHOLE-WHEAT APRICOT BREAD

These delicious small loaves make marvelous gifts.

1. Light oven and set it to 350° F (180° C).
2. Cut into small pieces and put in a mixing bowl:

    250 mL dried apricots   OR   150 g dried apricots
3. Add to apricots and set aside to cool:
    60 mL salad oil
    125 mL molasses         OR   164 g molasses
    160 mL boiling water

*Recipe continued on next page.*

4. In another bowl, mix together:
   250 mL whole-wheat flour   OR   130 g whole-wheat flour
   250 mL all-purpose flour   OR   120 g all-purpose flour
   1 mL baking soda
   10 mL baking powder
   10 mL salt
   250 mL chopped walnuts   OR   120 g chopped walnuts

5. When fruit mixture has cooled, add and mix:
   1 egg
   120 mL evaporated milk (canned)

6. Add fruit mixture to dry ingredients and mix only until you can't see the dry ingredients.
7. Grease 3 small loaf pans 9 cm x 15 cm.
8. Put batter in pans.
9. *Bake 45 minutes.* Remember the pans are *hot*, so use a pot holder. To test to see if the bread is done, put a toothpick into the center of the bread. If nothing clings to the toothpick when it is taken out, the bread is done.

NOT DONE    DONE

10. Cool loaves 10 minutes before removing from pan.
11. After loaves have cooled, wrap them in aluminum foil or plastic wrap and leave them overnight before slicing. The bread will be more moist.

*Recipe Makes:* 3 small loaves

# OTHER RECIPES

In this section you'll find recipes for beverages, uncooked jams, and other things you will enjoy making and eating.

# APPLE CRISP

The topping of this dessert is so good and crunchy.

1. Light oven and set it to 350° F (180° C).

2. Peel about 6 McIntosh apples, cut them into quarters, remove core, and slice them, to make:

   960 mL prepared apples    OR    480 g prepared apples

3. Put sliced apples in bottom of a baking dish about 2 L in size.
4. Sprinkle over the apples:
   5 mL cinnamon
   0.5 mL salt
5. Mix together thoroughly in a bowl:

   | | | |
   |---|---|---|
   | 75 mL flour | OR | 35 g flour |
   | 125 mL light brown sugar | OR | 100 g light brown sugar |
   | 125 mL dry oatmeal | OR | 35 g dry oatmeal |
   | 75 mL margarine | OR | 75 g margarine |

6. Spread the mixture evenly on top of the apples.
7. *Bake 40 minutes.* Remember the pan is *hot,* so use a pot

holder. The juice from the apples will bubble up through the topping, and the topping will be evenly browned when it is done.
8. Serve warm with milk or cream.

*Recipe Makes:* 6 servings

## GRANOLA-TYPE CEREAL

This makes a great snack as well as a breakfast cereal.

1. Light oven and set it to 350° F (180° C).
2. Mix together in a very large mixing bowl:

| | | |
|---|---|---|
| 1000 mL dry rolled oats | OR | 290 g dry rolled oats |
| 250 mL wheat germ | OR | 100 g wheat germ |
| 175 mL sliced almonds | OR | 70 g sliced almonds |
| 125 mL sesame seeds | OR | 70 g package sesame seeds |
| 125 mL flaked coconut | OR | 65 g flaked coconut |
| 125 mL light brown sugar | OR | 100 g light brown sugar |

2 mL salt
7 mL vanilla
120 mL water
180 mL salad oil

*Recipe continued on next page.*

3. Spread evenly on a broiler pan (without the grill) or any large, shallow pan.

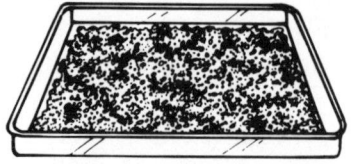

4. *Bake about 30 minutes.* Remember the pan is *hot,* so use a pot holder. Stir the mixture every 10 minutes to keep it from burning. The almonds will be nicely browned when the mixture is done.
5. After baking, stir in:
       250 mL white raisins     OR    130 g white raisins
6. Store in covered containers.

*Recipe Makes:* 2 L

# UNCOOKED RASPBERRY SPREAD*

This has a beautiful color and fresh flavor.

1. Wash two jelly glasses and sterilize them by covering them and their lids with water and boil 15 minutes. Remove glasses from water and cover with lids until ready to use, or leave in water until ready to use.
2. Thaw, put through a food mill or sieve to remove seeds, and then put in small electric mixer bowl:
    1 package frozen raspberries (283 g)
3. Stir into raspberries and let stand for 20 minutes, stirring occasionally:

            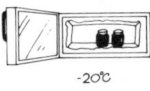

    350 mL sugar            OR     270 g sugar

4. Add and mix at lowest speed on electric mixer *for 3 minutes:*
    30 mL liquid pectin (Certo)
5. Pour spread into sterilized jelly glasses. Cover with lids and let stand at room temperature for 24 hours.
6. Store in refrigerator for use within 2 to 3 weeks, or put in the freezer for longer storage.

*Recipe Makes:* 2 glasses of spread

---

*Recipe based upon one developed at the College of Human Ecology at Cornell University

# UNCOOKED STRAWBERRY JAM*

This tastes like fresh strawberries and has a beautiful fresh color because it isn't cooked.

1. Wash three jelly glasses and sterilize them by covering them and their lids with water and boil 15 minutes. Remove glasses from water and cover with lids until ready to use, or leave in water until ready to use.
2. Mix in small bowl of electric mixer:
   1 package pectin (Sure Jel) (49 g)
   30 mL sugar
3. Put through a food mill or sieve, or blend in a blender:
   300 mL puréed fresh or
   unsweetened frozen
   strawberries
4. Add the strawberries to the small bowl of the electric mixer, and *mix* at lowest speed *for 7 minutes.*
5. Add and mix 3 minutes longer:

   175 mL sugar      OR      150 g sugar
   30 mL corn syrup
   10 mL lemon juice

6. Pour into jelly glasses and cover and let stand at room temperature for 24 hours.

---

*Recipe based upon one developed at the College of Human Ecology at Cornell University

7. Store in refrigerator for use within 2 to 3 weeks, or put in the freezer for longer storage.

*Recipe Makes:* 3 glasses of jam

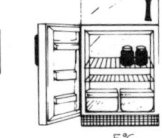

---

## FUDGE

---

This is beautifully smooth!

1. Grease a 20-cm square pan.
2. Put in a mixing bowl:

   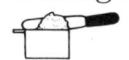 

   250 mL broken walnuts     OR    120 g broken walnuts

   1 package chocolate chips (170 g)
   5 mL vanilla
   125 mL margarine          OR    110 g margarine

3. Put in a saucepan and bring to a boil over medium heat, stirring *all the time* to prevent sticking:
   180 mL evaporated milk, canned
   500 mL sugar              OR    400 g sugar
   10 large marshmallows

   Be patient while the mixture comes to a boil (bubbles will break on the surface), then start timing and boil it for 6 minutes. Continue to stir it *all the time*. This is very hot, so be careful.
4. Carefully pour the hot mixture into the bowl with the chocolate and other ingredients. Stir it until margarine and chocolate chips melt.

*Recipe continued on next page.*

5. Pour the fudge into the greased square pan.
6. Allow it to cool and set in the refrigerator.
7. Cut into squares and remove from pan.

*Recipe Makes:* 25 pieces fudge

## HOT COCOA

This is good to warm you up on a cold day.

1. Mix together in a saucepan:
   15 mL cocoa
   30 mL sugar

2. Add and bring to a boil over medium heat while stirring:
   60 mL water

3. Add and continue to heat to the "right" temperature:
   480 mL milk

   Test for the "right" temperature by putting a small amount into a tasting spoon.

4. Serve immediately when it is hot enough for you.

*Recipe Makes:* 520 mL

# FRENCH CHOCOLATE

This is a marvelous treat!

1. Put in a pan and cook over medium heat, stirring all the time to prevent sticking:
   2½ squares baking chocolate
   80 mL water

2. Add and let come to a full boil while continuing to stir:

   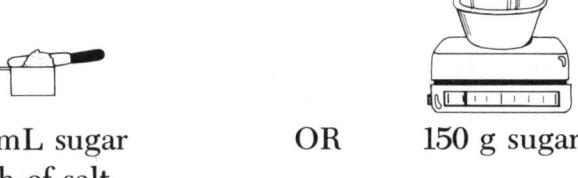

   175 mL sugar         OR         150 g sugar
   pinch of salt

3. Remove from the heat to cool. When cool, add:
   5 mL vanilla

4. In a bowl, beat until thick:
   250 mL heavy cream

5. When the chocolate mixture is cool to the touch (feel the outside of the pan; if it is cool, put a drop of the chocolate on your finger to test again), then gently stir the chocolate into the whipped cream. This chocolate mixture should be stored in a covered container in the refrigerator until used.

6. Heat the milk for the amount of hot chocolate you want.

*Recipe continued on next page.*

7. Put a generous spoonful of the chocolate mixture in a cup. Add the hot milk and stir.

*Recipe Makes:* 500 mL chocolate mixture (enough for 20 200-mL servings)

## ICED TEA

This is a delicious cooler on a hot day.

1. Bring to a boil:
   1 L water

2. Remove from heat and add:
   4 tea bags

   Let tea bags steep (stay) in the hot water 3 to 5 minutes. Then take out the tea bags.
3. Stir into the hot tea until it dissolves:

   125 mL sugar           OR      100 g sugar

4. Add and stir in:
   1 L water
   120 mL orange juice
   60 mL lemon juice
5. Serve over ice cubes.

   *Recipe Makes:* 9 240-mL servings

# Dinner Menus and Recipes for Beginners

It is easier for a beginning cook to start by cooking a recipe rather than a whole meal. But after gaining some experience in using kitchen utensils and cooking food, you'll be ready to prepare a meal. The following two menus with recipes provide a good way to get started.

Read the recipes and make a list of the foods you will need to buy.

Timing everything to be done at the same time takes planning. So carefully read the recipes and plan a schedule for when the different foods should be prepared. Include setting the table at a time when things are cooking and don't need watching. Put the schedule up where you can see what needs to be done next.

## MENU I

Meat Loaf
Baked Potatoes
Spinach
Apple Crisp
Milk

### Meat Loaf

1. Light oven and set it to 350° F (180° C).
2. Put in a bowl and mix thoroughly:

| 750 mL lean ground beef | OR | 750 g lean ground beef |

250 mL stewed tomatoes
| 175 mL dry bread crumbs | OR | 75 g dry bread crumbs |

1 egg
50 mL chopped onion
50 mL finely chopped celery
5 mL salt

*Recipe continued on next page.*

3. Put in a loaf pan.
4. *Bake 1 hour.*
5. Slice and serve.

*Recipe Makes:* 5 to 6 servings

## Baked Potato
1. Wash a baking potato for each person to be served.
2. Put on rack in oven and *bake 1 hour* with meat loaf [or bake at 400° F (200° C) if baking alone]. Potatoes are done if a kitchen fork can be inserted into them easily.
3. Cut a cross in the top of the potato. Press on the sides of the potato to open it up. Serve with salt and margarine.

## Spinach
1. Wash a 183-g package of fresh spinach, break off and discard large stems.
2. Put spinach in a large covered pan.
3. Drain spinach and cook in the water that clings to the leaves.
4. Add 1 mL salt.
5. Cook over medium heat. Stir once as the spinach starts to wilt.
6. *Cook* only until spinach wilts, *about 5 minutes.*
7. Drain spinach, and add 15 mL margarine.
8. Serve hot with lemon wedges.

*Recipe Makes:* 4 servings

**Apple Crisp**   For recipe, see page 00.

# MENU II

Sauteed Chicken Breasts
Baked Yams
Peas
Muffins
Fresh Fruit and Cookies
Milk

**Baked Yams**
1. Light oven and set it to 400° F (200° C).
2. Wash a yam for each person to be served.
3. *Bake for 1 hour* on rack in oven. Yams are done if a kitchen fork can be inserted into them easily.
4. Cut a cross in the top of the yam. Press on the sides of the yam to open it up. Serve with salt and margarine.

**Muffins**   For recipe, see page 64.

**Peas**

*This is the method you would use in cooking most frozen vegetables.*
1. Put in a covered saucepan:
    1 package frozen peas (183 g)
    25 mL water
    1 mL salt
2. *Boil* over medium heat (covered) until done *(about 10 minutes)*. The water should be almost evaporated at the end of the cooking time, but with such a small amount of water, you need to watch so that the peas do not boil dry and burn.
3. Add:
    15 mL margarine.
4. Serve hot.

*Recipe Makes:* 4 to 5 servings

### Sautéed Boned Chicken Breasts

1. Use ½ to 1 boned chicken breast for each person to be served. Cut off any solid white connective tissue on the chicken breast (connective tissue requires a longer cooking time and moisture to become tender).
2. Heat 25 mL margarine in a frying pan. Add chicken breasts. Cook over medium heat for about 5 *minutes*. Turn chicken and *cook 3 to 5 minutes more*. Cut a slit in a thick spot of the chicken to see if it is done. It should look white (or opaque), not like the uncooked chicken (translucent).
3. Salt and serve with lemon wedges.


**Fresh Fruit**   Serve fresh fruit that is in season (strawberries, blueberries, peaches, melon, etc.), or a combination of fruits sliced (banana, grapes without seeds, melon, etc.) and covered with a little orange juice.


**Cookies**   See recipes on pages 32-53. Make the day before, or before starting to prepare the meal.

# Kitchen Experiments

For budding scientists of school age, the following experiments will be fun. The experiments will show how carbon dioxide gas is formed from baking soda and baking powder to help baked products to rise and be light.

1. Cover the top of a table with unfolded newspapers. Then put 2 mL baking soda in each of 4 glass baking cups.
    Add 50 mL water to 3 of the cups.
   (No bubbles are formed since the baking soda needs some form of acid to form the bubbles of carbon dioxide.)
    Add 5 mL cream of tartar to one; 25 mL vinegar to another; and 25 mL lemon juice to another. Stir in 25 mL orange juice to the fourth cup with the baking soda.
   (With the addition of a food containing acid, the baking soda makes the bubbles that can be trapped by the dough and help the baked product to rise.)
    Baking soda + acid + water = carbon dioxide (gas)
2. Add 10 mL baking soda to 25 mL buttermilk in another glass cup.
   (Buttermilk is the acid used in many recipes, but the bubbles form more slowly and are not as dramatic.)
3. Put 50 mL water in another glass baking cup and add 5 mL baking powder.
   (These bubbles form because the baking powder includes both the acid and baking soda, as stated on the label.)
    Baking powder + water = carbon dioxide (gas)
   Now add 50 mL boiling water to the cup with the baking powder.
   (By heating the baking powder and water, more carbon dioxide is given off. This is what happens when muffins,

biscuits, etc. are heated as they bake. This is also why the baking powder is called "double acting." First the carbon dioxide is formed when liquid is added; and second, more carbon dioxide is formed when it is heated.)

Baking powder + water + heat = more carbon dioxide
(gas)

4. For a delicious experiment along this line, make the recipe for popovers on page 71. There is no baking soda or baking powder in popovers. They rise because the moisture in them is changed to steam as they bake. Steam takes up much more space than liquid, so the crusty shell of the flour and egg form around the steam, making the popover. Actually, the change of liquid into steam plays an important part in the rising of all baked products.

# Afterword for Adults

*Metric Cooking for Beginners* can be a help to anyone who is beginning to use metric measurements in cooking. However, the recipes in this book have been written with the beginning cook in mind. Younger school children are already using metric units in measurements, so they may be more familiar with the metric terms than adults. I have included many helps for the beginning cook of either elementary school or junior high age. A young person will need the supervision of someone with some cooking experience for safety in using electric equipment and the oven or stove. The very youngest will need help in reading and cooking techniques. Older children and young people who already have some cooking experience can successfully follow the recipes once they understand how to measure and weigh ingredients.

## *About the Recipes*

The flour used in the recipes is all-purpose, unless otherwise specified; baking powder is double-acting; and margarine instead of butter is called for, in recognition of the fact that there is a need to control the amount of animal fat in our food. Furthermore, you should try to buy margarine with a high proportion of polyunsaturated fats. Since polyunsaturated fats tend to be in liquid form, look for margarine labels showing that "liquid . . . oil" is the first ingredient listed.

Choose a margarine that has a flavor you like. Soft margarine, rather than that sold in sticks, is so easy to mix that I suggest you try it. Do not use margarines labelled "diet," "whipped," or "spread." However, butter could be substituted for margarine if you wish. Salad oil is called for in several recipes. This means one without flavor, preferably corn oil.

## *Measurement By Volume Vs Mass (Weight)*

In changing to metric measures for cooking, the American Home Economics Association has selected the method of measuring dry ingredients by volume as the standard for the American people. The AHEA felt that the public would find the shift to metrics easier if they only had to learn new metric terms for volume and not the new measuring technique of weighing as well. Also, the cost of the change would be less than if a scale had to be purchased.

However, the *Handbook for Metric Usage* published by the AHEA states, "The mass method, commonly used in many large quantity food service centers and in homes in some European countries is more accurate, easier and faster to use for some ingredients than the volume method."[1] And in *The Cooks' Catalogue* by James Beard and others, the authors state, "Measuring by weight is both more exact and more sensible than measuring by volume or number."[2] I have used metric measurements in cooking for years and our children find the weighing of ingredients much faster and better than measuring by volume.

Weighing ingredients is more accurate because a given mass (weight) doesn't change whether it is packed down, piled on lightly, or sifted—in contrast to the wide variations that can occur when ingredients are measured by volume. Also, a recipe can be more exact because it can call for weighing any amount rather than being limited to combinations of the standard measuring containers for volume.

It is easier and faster because a given amount can be poured out rather than measuring one or more containers to overflowing and then leveling them off with a knife. In the case of flour, there is no need to stir or sift it in order to get a standard measure. In the case of fat, it is less messy and easier to weigh out a given amount right into a lightweight mixing bowl. There are also fewer items to wash, since the dry measuring containers are not needed. The simplicity of this method makes it more attractive to the beginner. To an experienced cook, the speed and ease of measuring by weight seems just one step removed from the ease of preparing a "mix." It is an especially useful method for measuring the larger quantities of dry

---

1. American Home Economics Association, *Handbook for Metric Usage* (Washington: 1977), p. 12.
2. Beard, Glasser, Wolf, Ltd., *The Cooks' Catalogue* (New York: Harper, 1975), p. 9.

ingredients for baked products such as cookies, cakes, breads, etc.

When a new method of measuring is found to be more accurate, easier and faster than an existing method, I feel it should be presented as an alternative to be judged on its own merit. Therefore, the recipes given in this book permit a choice in the method of measuring the dry ingredients.

## *Terminology*

The American Home Economics Association has set standards for metric usage in the areas of home economics based on those set by the National Bureau of Standards and the American National Metric Council. The terminology in this book is consistent with the AHEA *Handbook of Metric Usage.*

The spelling of *liter* and *meter* is preferred by these organizations, although *litre* and *metre* are used by some organizations in the U.S., since it is the international standard.

The symbol for liter chosen by these groups is $L$, since the lower case l can be confused with the numeral 1 on the typewriter. To be consistent with this, the symbol for milliliter is $mL$. These symbols have been selected by the organizations mentioned above and may at first seem strange to those adults who have not studied science recently.

Mass is the term used to measure the quantity of matter in an object. We use the familiar term *weight* for this. However, in science, *weight* has another meaning—the force of gravity. However, there are no good substitutes in ordinary language for the words "weigh" and "weight," so we have used them along with the proper term "mass."

## *How to Change Conventional Measures to Metric Unit*

You may want to change measurements of ingredients in recipes that call for standard cups so that you can weigh them on a metric scale. To help you do this, here are the weights of basic ingredients. For other items called for in your recipes, measure them once in the standard cup. Then weigh that amount on the metric scale and write down the weight in grams. Then the measurements in your recipe will have been changed for easy weighing.

*All-purpose flour*
1 cup   = 120 g
¾ cup =   90 g
½ cup =   60 g
¼ cup =   30 g

*Sugar, granulated or light brown*
1 cup   = 200 g
¾ cup = 150 g
½ cup = 100 g
¼ cup =   50 g

*Margarine or butter*
1 cup   = 220 g
¾ cup = 165 g
½ cup = 110 g
¼ cup =   55 g

*Hydrogenated fat*
1 cup   = 180 g
¾ cup = 135 g
½ cup =   90 g
¼ cup =   45 g

In order to change liquid measures to milliliters, you need to know that:
1 cup            = 240 mL (actually 236.6, but 240 is close enough)
1 tablespoon = 15 mL
1 teaspoon    = 5 mL

# Manufacturers of Metric Measuring Utensils and Scales

It might be helpful to know some of the manufacturers of the metric measures and scales. Prices change fairly rapidly but the prices given below will provide you with some comparisons among items as well as among manufacturers.

### Dry-Metric Measure Sets
The standard is a set of three containers marked 50 mL, 125 mL, and 250 mL.
*Foley Manufacturing Co.* makes a stainless steel set for $3.49. They also have cups marked with the exact conversions of the conventional cups, so make sure you are getting the standard containers mentioned above.
*Ohaus Scale Corporation* makes a standard metric set in plastic for $1.50. They are not primarily manufacturers of household utensils, but have an outstanding line of metric teaching aids.

### Metric Spoon Sets
The standard is a set of five spoons marked 1 mL, 2 mL, 5 mL, 15 mL, and 25 mL.
*Ohaus Scale Corporation* makes this standard set of metric spoons in plastic for $.75.

### Liquid Measures
*Corning Glass Works* makes Pyrex measures in three sizes: 250-mL size for $1.09, 500-mL size for $1.49, and 1,000-mL size for $1.99.
*Foley Manufacturing Co.* makes a plastic 250-mL measure for $1.19, and a 500-mL size for $1.49.
*Ohaus Scale Corporation* makes a plastic 1,000-mL size for $5.95 marked in 10-mL divisions.

## Scales

*Aikenwood Corporation* distributes a variety of Salter scales, priced from $10 to $40. The Weighmix 37, at $30, was selected as a "Best Buy" by *Consumer Reports* in the November 1976 issue.

*John Chatillon & Sons, Inc.* makes an institutional-style (accurate, reliable, but large) scale with a 5-kilogram capacity for $50.00.

*Metric-Aids/Dick Blick* supplies a scale with a 5-kilogram capacity for $15.60.

*Ohaus Scale Corporation* makes a platform-spring scale with a 5-kilogram capacity for $12.50.

*Selective Educational Equipment, Inc.* supplies a scale with a 4.5-kilogram capacity for $11.00.

*Terraillon Corporation* makes a variety of scales priced from $17 to $21. The BA2000, with a 2-kilogram capacity is $18. It was chosen as part of the Permanent Design Collection of the Museum of Modern Art.

## *Addresses for Manufacturers and Distributors*

Aikenwood Corporation
2151 Park Blvd.
Palo Alto, CA 94302

John Chatillon & Sons, Inc.
83-30 Kew Gardens Road
Kew Gardens, NY 11415

Corning Glass Works
Corning, NY 14830

Foley Manufacturing Co.
Housewares Division
3300 N. E. 5th Street
Minneapolis, MN 55418

Metric-Aids/Dick Blick
P.O. Box 1267
Galesburg, IL 61401

Ohaus Scale Corporation
29 Hanover Road
Florham Park, NJ 07932

Selective Educational Equipment, Inc.
3 Bridge Street
Newton, MA 02195

Terraillon Corporation
95 Q South Hoffman Lane
Central Islip, NY 11722

For your convenience, a complete package of metric utensils and a scale are available from the author. For a price list write to Ginevera Barta, P.O. Box 507, Chatham, N.J. 07928.

# Recipe Index

Apple Crisp 74

Banana Bread 55
Biscuits 57
Buttermilk Pancakes 59

Chicken Breasts, Boned and
    Sautéed 86
Coffee Cake 61
Cocoa 80
Cookies
    Brownies 29
    Butterscotch Brownies 30
    Chocolate Chip 32
    Chocolate-Chip Meringue 34
    Date Bars 36
    Date-Nut Meringue 38
    Ginger 40
    Peanut-Butter 41
    Refrigerator Date
        Pinwheels 43
    Refrigerator Oatmeal 46
    Rolled Sugar 48
    Sesame Seed 50
    Soft Sugar 52

French Chocolate 81

Fudge 79

Granola-Type Cereal 75
Grapenut Bread 62

Iced Tea 82

Meat Loaf 83
Muffins 64
    Blueberry Muffins 66
    Cranberry Muffins 68

Peas, frozen 85
Popovers 70
Potato, Baked 84

Spinach 84

Uncooked Raspberry Spread 77
Uncooked Strawberry Jam 78

Whole-Wheat Apricot Bread 71

Yams, Baked 85